Brad Stevens: The Inspiring Life and Leadership Lessons of One of Basketball's Greatest Young Coaches

An Unauthorized Biography & Leadership Case Study

By: Clayton Geoffreys

Table of Contents

Foreword

Often times when college-level coaches make the jump to coaching in the NBA, their success is not nearly comparable to their previous NCAA accomplishments. The college game is fundamentally very different from the NBA. However, once every now and then, a college coach is able to make a seamless and immediate transition to the big leagues. The latest of college coaches to successfully make the jump is Boston Celtics head coach, Brad Stevens. In the summer of 2013, Brad Stevens shocked the basketball world by leaving the esteemed Butler program he played a pivotal role building, to join one of the NBA's most storied franchises, the Boston Celtics. Since then, Stevens has emerged as one of the best coaches in the league, leading the Boston Celtics to several playoff bids and in 2017, a return to the Eastern Conference Finals. Still a very young coach in the league, Stevens has quickly established himself as a premier coach, demanding the respect of many league veteran coaches such as Gregg Popovich. It will be exciting to see what Stevens is able to accomplish in the years ahead. Thank you for purchasing *Brad Stevens: The Inspiring Life and Leadership Lessons of One of Basketball's Greatest Young Coaches*. In this unauthorized biography and leadership case study, we will learn some of the background behind Brad's incredible life story, and more importantly his impact on the game of basketball. In the last section of the book, we'll learn what makes Brad such an effective leader and coach, including a review of key takeaways that you can remember when looking to apply lessons from Brad to your own life. Hope you enjoy and if you do, please do not forget to leave a review!

Also, check out my website at claytongeoffreys.com to join my exclusive list where I let you know about my latest books. To thank you for your purchase, you can go to my site to download a free copy of *33 Life Lessons: Success Principles, Career Advice & Habits of Successful People*. In the book, you'll learn from some of the greatest thought leaders of different industries on what it takes to become successful and how to live a great life.

Cheers,

Clayton Geoffreys

Visit me at www.claytongeoffreys.com

Introduction

They say that being a coach is about having the experience of being able to play and experience what it is like to be on an NBA court where basketball is played at its highest level. It is always different when you have experienced the hard grind and difficulty of going through an NBA season, and then you try to preach it to players that are also trying to carve out their NBA careers.

Some of the more successful players turned NBA coaches include the 11-time NBA champion coach Phil Jackson, who was part of the 1972-73 championship roster of the New York Knicks. He would soon become an assistant for the Chicago Bulls in the 80's before he took the reins as the head coach and won six titles for them in the 90's. He then would win five more titles for the Los Angeles Lakers during the 2000's era.

Many other former NBA players that have found themselves coaching teams in the big league. These include Bill Russell (who once played for the Celtics, but ended up coaching them after), Larry Bird (who played for Boston but coached the Pacers later on), and Doc Rivers (who was a key part of the Hawks in the 80's and won a title with the Celtics as a coach). Byron Scott was a key member of the Showtime Lakers, who would coach the New Orleans Hornets and the Lakers soon afterward, among others.

It is those coaches' experience as NBA players that have provided the knowledge and know-how they needed to become successful in their endeavors as strategists in the league. Their personnel can relate to what they have experienced as former players, and that is an aspect of coaching that has been difficult to replace. They know what it takes to manage a grinding NBA season and probably even a title run.

However, there are also successful coaches that have never even had a chance to play in the NBA, but have nevertheless become successful because of the experience they got working under great coaches. One name that comes to mind is Gregg Popovich, who never played in the NBA, but has had the opportunity to become an assistant to some legendary coaches.

Popovich, or "Pop," as he is often called, initially worked under Larry Brown with the San Antonio Spurs as an assistant before he moved to Golden State to work with Don Nelson. Upon his return to San Antonio, he assumed the role as the GM before naming himself the coach of the Spurs. He has been the head coach of the Spurs since 1996. He would go on to win five titles in San Antonio.

There is also Erik Spoelstra, who started from a video job in the Miami Heat but would later win two NBA titles coaching LeBron James, Dwyane Wade, and Chris Bosh. You could also include Tom Thibodeau and Mike Budenholzer, who were both good enough as coaches to lead their respective teams to 60 wins in a season. Both coaches have had the pleasure of working under some of the best minds in the NBA before assuming their current jobs.

While experience playing in the NBA or working under a good coach prove to be invaluable for one looking to become a head coach himself in the big leagues, those are not necessarily what defines them. Doctors and dentists do not necessarily need to get sick or get toothaches to become the best in their respective fields. Nor do they need years of experience as assistants under established doctors and dentists to excel immediately. The same can be said about NBA head coaches.

The NBA has seen its fair share of coaches that have not had the chance of playing in the league professionally, nor work as assistants under established head coaches in some teams. All they needed was to show early potential as a future head coach for teams and executives to consider what they could provide as the man leading a group of players from the bench. One such notable name that comes to mind is Brad Stevens.

Brad Stevens grew up loving the game of basketball. He also ended up playing college basketball albeit in a less competitive league. However, he was aware that he was not much of a basketball player. He knew he was not going to get far with the skills he had. Instead, Stevens relied on his smarts to get to where he is. Brad Stevens took an academic route to get to the position he is right now as compared to coaches that relied more on experience.

After graduating from an academically prestigious university as a regular honor student, Brad Stevens would work for a well-known pharmaceutical company considering he was a degree holder of economics. However, he got the opportunity to volunteer for the Butler University Bulldogs basketball team teaching summer basketball camps, which convinced him to take a different career route.

During the 2000-01 season in Butler, then-coach Thad Matta offered Stevens a job as a basketball coordinator for the team. It would not take long for Brad Stevens to prove his pedigree and potential as a coach. New head coach Todd Lickliter would name Stevens as one of his assistants just a season after the latter worked as a coordinator. It was during this time when Brad Stevens became a more active member of the Butler Bulldogs.

After six seasons working under Lickliter, Brad Stevens would get promoted to the head coach's job after the former coach resigned to take a job elsewhere. The decision came when the members of the team urged the executives to promote a former assistant that already knew the system and culture of the school.

Stevens was the lucky candidate despite being barely over the age of 30.

Throughout his years as Butler's head coach, Brad Stevens was constantly one of the youngest strategists among all the Division I schools. Despite his youth, Stevens never showed any difficulties in transitioning from being an assistant. He showed smarts and strategies that would have belied his youth and inexperience as a head coach. In only his first season as Butler's head coach, he would win the Horizon League title and lead the team to a seventh seed in the NCAA Tournament.

Brad Stevens would reach as far as the NCAA championship game as the head coach of the Butler Bulldogs twice during his tenure. The first time was in 2010, while the second appearance came a year later. A few years later, he became a hot commodity as several other Division I schools were trying to win him over to their side. Whatever they offered him could not sway Stevens because he was meant for bigger things.

Stevens would decline several job opportunities with different NCAA schools because he was going to places where the grass was greener. In 2013, Brad Stevens accepted the offer to become the head coach of the Boston Celtics, who were in the middle of a rebuilding period after moving on from the Big Three era. Because of his youth, Stevens was chosen to be the one to head-start what was thought to be an extended rebuilding period.

It would not take long for Brad Stevens to make some noise in the NBA. In as early as his second season as the head coach, he would lead the Boston Celtics to a playoff appearance, though the team did not have any big name stars that most postseason teams had. Two years later, he would find himself coaching the 2017 Eastern All-Stars after leading the Boston Celtics to what was then the East's best record. He would end the

2016-17 season leading the Celtics to the top seed in the Eastern Conference.

In only a few seasons in the NBA, Brad Stevens has already become one of the best coaches in the league, though nobody would expect his team to compete as hard as they did. Despite their youth and inexperience, the so-called rebuilding Celtics have become a contender in the East because of Brad Stevens' way of preaching toughness and team play.

But what has become a surprise to everyone is that Stevens was not even an NBA player to begin with. He did not play for a Division I college, nor was he an assistant for an established NBA coach. He started from scratch as a coordinator all the way to becoming a head coach for Butler. And when he got to the NBA, he knew practically nothing about it aside from what he had read and heard. But despite that, Brad Stevens has proven that one can always take a different path to reach the same kind of success that those that have taken the conventional road have reached.

Chapter 1: Background

Throughout Brad Stevens' journey from a young boy that loved the game of basketball to a top coach in the NBA, the recurring theme that has brought him to the dance as the bench leader of one of the most storied franchises in the history of the league is his hard work. Of course, the roots of his hard working mentality started in Indiana, one of the craziest states when it comes to the game of basketball.

Brad Stevens was born on October 22, 1976, in Greensville, South Carolina. However, his family would move to Zionsville, Indiana four years later. While it is common knowledge that Indiana loves basketball probably more than any other place in America, Brad Stevens was lucky enough to be born during an era when the game ruled the state. This made it easy for a young child like Brad Stevens to fall in love with the game.

First off, the legendary college head coach Bob Knight had already planted himself as the mainstay of the Indiana University Hoosiers, one of the top Division I NCAA schools in the country. Stevens was born during the year when Knight won his first NCAA title in 1976. He would go on to win two more titles during his tenure with the Hoosiers. Pretty soon, Indiana would be known as the Hoosier State thanks in part to how Knight was helping his team dominate their conference.

Brad Stevens was an avid fan of Bob Knight and the Indiana Hoosiers. As early as his kindergarten years, Stevens would watch tapes of Hoosier basketball games with his father during the afternoons. He would also often get a glimpse of the Hoosiers in person when he and his father, Dr. Mark Stevens, would decide to drive an hour and a half to Bloomington, where Indiana University played.

Stevens' years as a child was characterized by his daily routine of playing basketball outside on the family's driveway. Pretty soon, he and other neighborhood kids would find themselves playing in a court installed in the backyard of one of his friends. Brad Stevens learned the value of hard work early at this stage of his life playing against and with friends in a rural town in the blue collar state of Indiana.

Reed Taylor, who would soon become Stevens' AAU coach, recalled how hard Brad Stevens worked every single game. At that time, Stevens was still in fourth grade. What he noticed about the young boy was that he would always sprint back on offense as soon as he saw someone getting a rebound. That gave him an opportunity to get a quick bucket. Taylor said Stevens was not the fastest kid on the floor. However, he outworked everyone else in getting to the other end before the defense could get settled.[ii]

Another one of the characteristics that Taylor saw in Stevens was that he was always calm and collected amidst the pressure and intensity of the games. He was never too tense and always kept his cool. This was a trait that Brad Stevens would bring all the way to his years as a head coach. You would never see him screaming at the sidelines or lose his cool and show his temper during botched plays or blown calls.

And during Brad Stevens' early teen years right before he went to high school, he went a level further by becoming an avid fan of the Indiana Pacers. At that time, the Pacers had Reggie Miller gunning and draining three-pointers for Indiana. At that point in his career, Stevens was much like Reggie Miller as far as style was concerned. He was an avid fan of the three-point shot. At one point, Stevens even had the bravado to challenge Miller to a shootout.

Brad Stevens was in middle school when Reggie Miller visited the young basketball fans and players of

Zionsville. Miller would ask the kids if they wanted to challenge him to a shootout. No other middle school kid stood up except for Brad Stevens. Of course, the NBA player Reggie Miller won out against the middle school boy.[i] But that experience showed how tough and confident of a person Brad Stevens was, even when he was a kid.

After that short and memorable experience with Reggie Miller, Brad Stevens would go on to attend Zionsville Community High School. Knowing that his shooting was his ticket to a varsity roster spot, Stevens would always get up early for morning shoot-around and shooting practices at a nearby local basketball court before school started. And when he finally got the roster spot he worked so hard for, he decided to wear the number 31 like Reggie Miller did when he played for the Pacers.

By the time Brad Stevens reached his sophomore year, he was a star for the Zionsville Eagles, who went all the way to the sectional finals of the state of Indiana. But the finals of that season, as Stevens himself would say, remains to be the worst memory he has had in his career in sports. The Eagles were up eight points with barely two minutes left. Then their opponents, the Lebanon Tigers, roared back to tie the game at 59 with merely seconds remaining. And when the buzzer hit, a shot from the Tigers found itself down the net in what was a miraculous 10-run for them to defeat the Eagles.[ii]

That memory kept Brad Stevens fired up and motivated throughout the following season. The Zionsville Eagles were in the middle near-decade drought for a sectional title. Giving his school the pleasure and prestige of winning a title again for the first time since 1986 was what kept Brad Stevens going, even after that painful loss to the Lebanon Tigers a year before.

But Brad Stevens did not have to work harder than he ever did, nor did he even have to be so passionate about basketball. While other kids had no choice but to use basketball as their means to escape what would have been a dark future, Stevens had everything going for him. He was a student that excelled in almost all facets of academic life. He had good grades, was a member of numerous athletic programs, and was an active student council member. Simply put, Stevens could have excelled in almost any endeavor he put his mind to. He did not need to be so passionate about the game of basketball.[ii]

Brad Stevens' passion for basketball would be compounded with the help of one of the team's assistants, Phil Isenbarger. Isenbarger was a member of one of Indiana University's championship teams back in the 80's. After his years as a college basketball player, he would go on to become a lawyer. However, Isenbarger's passion for basketball never wavered even after becoming a lawyer. He would remain one of the more passionate assistants for the Eagles. He became a role model for Stevens to become so hard working and passionate about the game.[ii]

It would take until his senior year for Brad Stevens to finally lead his team to the sectional title against North Montgomery, the school that sent them packing a season back. Stevens was hot the entire game, scoring 33 points and getting named the Sectional MVP in that win. He would leave the team setting school records for nearly all aspects of the game. He still holds the record for most points, assists, and steals for the school. Stevens finished averaging over 32 points per game during his senior year in sectional play.

Despite starring for three years at Zionsville Community High School, Brad Stevens' skills remained modest and may have even peaked by then. His dream was to play for Bob Knight at Indiana University. He was always a big fan of the Hoosiers. He grew up watching them as a child. If not the Hoosiers, he was also open to playing for Butler

University. However, none of those Division I schools wanted him. No offers were made.

Bill Hodges, who was known as the Larry Bird's coach at Indiana State, believed that Brad Stevens was good enough to immediately play for Mercer University as a freshman because he thought he had the same kind of basketball IQ as the legendary Celtic did. However, Stevens opted to decline the only Division I school that offered him a scholarship.[ii]

Mercer University was too far away from home for Brad Stevens. On top of that, he always knew his limitations as a basketball player. Stevens was not the tallest guard, nor was he very athletic. His skills were modest at best despite his strong passion and love for the game of basketball. Instead, he would go and choose the academic route while also playing basketball. Brad Stevens decided to go to DePauw University. He knew that there was life after basketball, and that was the very reason why he chose DePauw.

Stevens wanted to prepare himself for what was to come after his years as a basketball player.

When Brad Stevens joined DePauw, he was not a star. He was a reserved guard on the basketball team. However, his love for the game of basketball never diminished, even when he was a nominee for the Academic-All America year after year for his distinguished efforts in both his academic studies and his athletic endeavors. What set him apart during his college years was not his skills on the basketball court, but his ability to juggle working hard for the team every single day while studying diligently for his exams.

Unlike most college players, who would more than likely excel more a season later, Brad Stevens was different. He had good moments when he was a freshman. When he was a sophomore, he was the team's second-leading scorer. It was the same thing the following year. Stevens was producing fairly well, and yet the team was losing more than they expected they would. Bill Fenlon, DePauw's head coach, would make adjustments. He would give more emphasis to developing his younger and more talented players. Brad Stevens' minutes diminished year after year.[iii]

Of course, Brad Stevens had no reason to be happy about his reduced minutes. Nobody wanted to see less time even though he believed his production was good enough for steady minutes. But Stevens learned a valuable lesson because of this. As Fenlon would put it, a good teammate knows how to accept his role. Acceptance is different from liking or satisfaction, but Fenlon nonetheless stressed to his players how important acceptance is when it comes to a team setup.

Despite learning how to accept his role, Brad Stevens could not handle getting fewer minutes than his freshmen counterparts did. It hurt his ego. At that brief moment in his career as a basketball player, he thought about quitting the game he worked so hard for. It was easy for him to think about it at that time. The team was losing game after game. Quitting was also a viable option for him because he already had a good corporate job waiting for him after graduation. But it was a job and life without basketball. If there were even any, they would be minimal at best.[iii]

While Brad Stevens never dreamed of being in the NBA or making it to the big stage of basketball at the Olympics, he was still down about getting benched. Basketball was not fun for him at that point in his college career. There seemed to be no point in continuing with something that was not making him happy anymore. But then again, he was too far into the sport to just suddenly quit. Stevens thought he would regret it if he did not finish strong with the team. Pretty soon after that during his senior year, he would start some games while owning the leadership role as the captain of the team.

One memory that Brad Stevens had that made him a better leader overall was during practice. He would lead the team's second unit against a starting team full of younger players. He and some other bench players torched the starting squad and were even talking a little smack. After the practice, Fenlon called him up to his office. Stevens expected his coach to praise him and to tell him that he would be getting more minutes. Instead, Fenlon scolded him and the bench players for what he perceived as Stevens' way of tearing down the starters. For Fenlon, Brad Stevens was a leader that was supposed to get his teammates' confidence up. Instead, he buried them deep after that practice session.[iii]

For a young man as competitive and hard working as Brad Stevens was, that message did not sit in well with him. Despite that, he did not let his personal feelings get in the way of their locker room chemistry. But Stevens would view that moment in his life as a time he had to endure until graduation. It would remain that way until several years later when he was already a coach. Brad Stevens recalled how he discovered so much of himself back then when he showed his true colors. But for him, it was the decision to stay with the team and work hard that mattered most in such a trying time in his career.[iii]

Brad Stevens would graduate from DePauw University averaging only a little more than five points per game during his senior year. Most of his career in DePauw was highlighted by the fact that he was an outstanding student-athlete that excelled in academics and sports. He was a three-time Academic-All America nominee and had earned several all-academic conference awards. He graduated as a member of the Dean's List with a degree in Economics.

After graduating from DePauw in 1999, Brad Stevens would get a secure corporate job as a marketing associate for Eli Lilly, a pharmaceutical firm. However, there was no basketball involved with that kind of a job. During some days, Brad Stevens would feel as if basketball was still calling for him even after he had already left the game at DePauw.

But the inevitable happened. Brad Stevens was offered a job as a volunteer assistant on Butler University's basketball team. Then, he was later given a full-time job. He started off as a coordinator doing administrative duties that mostly involved compiling and editing video clips—a job that took more than half of his day. The most painful part about it was that the pay was painfully low for someone of Brad Stevens' academic background.

During the 2001-02 season, former assistant coach Todd Lickliter took over former head coach Thad Matta's job. Lickliter was one of the assistants that saw how hard Stevens worked as a coordinator. He never knew how difficult a job Brad Stevens was doing until he tried it himself. But Stevens made it look easy and never complained about it, even though he was getting paid a meager sum of money. He would give the hard working young man a slot in his staff as an assistant coach.

Brad Stevens would work under Todd Lickliter as an assistant for six seasons. He was one of the more active assistants in Lickliter's staff. However, Stevens' fate would take a quick turn for the better when Lickliter resigned in 2007 to take a job as the new head coach of the University of Iowa. This opened up Butler's head coaching position for anyone to take. Brad Stevens was one of the top candidates.

Chapter 2: Coaching at Butler

After Lickliter had left Butler for Iowa, the head coaching position opened up for all of the team's assistant coaches at the request of the players to promote one of them to the post. Of course, the young 30-year-old Brad Stevens was one of those interviewed for the job. In due time, Stevens was named the replacement for Lickliter and the new head coach of the Butler Bulldogs. It only took the athletic director three days to make the decision to hire the young former assistant.[iv]

What made the decision easy for Butler athletic director Barry Collier was that despite Brad Stevens' youth and inexperience, he had spent the previous six seasons working as an assistant and learning the system and the culture itself. Butler has been successful for quite a long time by promoting assistant coaches that have learned the system inside-out. Brad Stevens was only continuing what had started when

Collier himself promoted his former assistant Thad Matta to become the head coach of the Butler Bulldogs.[iv]

Collier believed that Brad Stevens, at his age, already understood the Butler way after seven years of working for the team. He knew that Stevens had to make certain decisions that would not necessarily be the same as what the former coaches would do, but he nevertheless believed that the system would stay as it was and would continue under the young head coach. He also saw how Brad Stevens shined under Lickliter and how he related to the players. He always had a good relationship with the players and the entire staff as well.[iv]

But the pressure was on for Brad Stevens. Other than getting a lot of attention and heat for being the second-youngest head coach in Division I basketball at that time, he was also going to have to build on what was a school record for victories the past season. It was either he was going to improve on that milestone, or he was going to allow the Bulldogs to plummet down from what was perceived to be their best season at that time.

Brad Stevens would immediately exceed all expectations the moment he put on the head coach's jacket. Stevens led the Bulldogs to an 8-0 start to the season having defeated Texas Tech, a team coached by Bob Knight who he spent hours watching tapes as a child when he was still coaching Indiana University. This led Knight himself to say that the Butler Bulldogs under Brad Stevens played with a lot of smartness. Other head coaches believed that what got Butler to an early 12-1 start to the season was the toughness that Stevens instilled in them.

After that blistering hot start to the season for Brad Stevens and his Bulldogs, one cannot help but praise how he was so quick to make the jump from assistant to head coach. He was often described as calm and composed on the sidelines as if he had been a veteran head coach for several years already. Even Collier himself was impressed at how Stevens remained the same guy he was when he was still an assistant. He was never too tense. Stevens always kept a composed demeanor on the sidelines to show how fit for the job as a head coach he was.[v]

After a record-setting previous season for the Butler Bulldogs, Brad Stevens took the team a step further by finishing the season with a record of 27-3. They would qualify for the NCAA Tournament by winning the Horizon League championship. The team would make it as far as the second round of March Madness after beating South Alabama in the first round. They would fall to Tennessee in the second round after a tough overtime game. After that season, Stevens nearly won the National Coach of the Year award after becoming the third-youngest head coach in Division I history to lead a team to a total of 30 wins in a season.

The following season, the Butler Bulldogs would be ranked fifth in the Horizon League during the preseason primarily because they lost four starters. But Brad Stevens exceeded expectations yet again by finishing first in the conference, though they would lose the Horizon League championship to Cleveland State. Nevertheless, Butler was given the ninth seed in the NCAA Tournament, but would lose in the first round to Louisiana State. Brad Stevens would finish the season winning the Horizon League Coach of the Year and was a finalist for the National Coach of the Year award again.

Heading into the 2009-10 season, the Butler Bulldogs were seen as favorites for the national title because of how two key players gained valuable experience over the summer. Gordon Hayward and Shelvin Mack, the two outstanding freshmen from the previous season, won the gold medal in the FIBA Under-19 Tournament during the summer.

However, the Bulldogs would start slow and would begin the season with a 9-4 record. Despite the unfortunate start, Brad Stevens would lead the team to 16 straight wins. After those 16 wins, the Bulldogs would beat Siena and would give Brad Stevens a record-tying victory. With 81 wins in his first three seasons, Brad Stevens tied Mark Few for most wins by a Division I head coach in a span of three years. A week later, he broke the record after completing his 18th straight win in the conference. Stevens and Butler would advance to the NCAA Tournament after winning the Horizon League championship. Butler was 20-0 during conference play. With that accomplishment, Stevens was the only coach that season to sweep his entire conference.

Brad Stevens would lead the team as far as the NCAA Championship Game that season after recording 25 straight wins spanning from conference play up to March Madness. The Bulldogs faced heavy competition along the way. They qualified for the Elite

Eight by beating the top-seeded Syracuse Oranges. They would then reach the Final Four by downing Kansas State. And with that win against Kansas State, Brad Stevens became the youngest head coach to reach the Final Four since Bob Knight did it in 1973. Stevens was 33 at that time while Knight did it at the age of 32.

Using tough defense, Brad Stevens led the Butler Bulldogs to a victory over Michigan State in the semi-finals to reach the NCAA Tournament Finals. Because of that, Brad Stevens became the youngest head coach to reach the National Championship Game in seven decades. However, Butler would eventually lose to Duke University by two points in the title game to finish the season as the second-best team in the entire nation. For the third straight season, Stevens would be a finalist for the National Coach of the Year award. And after such a miracle run to the title game, Brad Stevens had already made himself known as one of the brightest young minds in coaching history.

The following season, the Butler Bulldogs would have been favorites to reach the NCAA Finals again, but they would fall far from what was expected of them early on after they struggled due to the loss of Gordon Hayward, who had tried his hand at the NBA already. Nevertheless, the Bulldogs would still manage to win the Horizon League title to make the NCAA Tournament.

During the first two rounds of March Madness, it would take clutch plays for Brad Stevens and his Butler Bulldogs to win games against Old Dominion and Pitt. They would even make it as far as the NCAA Finals again with dramatic wins over Wisconsin, Florida, and VCU. However, Stevens and his Bulldogs would fall yet again in the championship game. This time, it was against Connecticut.

The following year, the Bulldogs would fail to win the Horizon League title and would finish third in their conference. They would not even make it to the

NCAA Tournament. However, Brad Stevens still managed to lead them as far as the semis of the College Basketball Invitational. It would then also be the final year for Butler to play in the Horizon League.

During the 2012-13 season, Butler would move over to the Atlantic 10 Conference, which was thought to be tougher than the Horizon League. Despite being new to the conference, Brad Stevens managed to lead his team to 26 wins and a third-place finish in the A-10. Butler would make it as far as the semis of the A-10 Tournament, but they would ultimately fall short of making it to the championship game. That season would turn out to be Brad Stevens' final year with the Butler Bulldogs.

After the 2012-13 season, Brad Stevens would get an offer from the Boston Celtics to become their new head coach. It was not a shock for Stevens to get an offer from another basketball team. After all, he had been getting bigger offers from other Division I schools since leading Butler to an NCAA Finals appearance in 2010. However, he had dismissed all of those proposals, claiming that he loved being loyal to Butler, which he thought was a unique school that had a good tradition in basketball.

But the Boston Celtics were not any ordinary basketball team. The Celtics, along with the Lakers, is arguably the most storied franchise in the history of the basketball world. Seventeen championship banners say so. With that kind of a rich history spanning from the 50's, and with a supportive fanbase backing the team up, most anyone would want to coach or play for such a historic basketball team in the NBA. Brad Stevens would be no exception.

Brad Stevens would have breakfast with several of the Boston Celtics' top executives to discuss the possibility of him coaching the team. Danny Ainge of the Celtics had been trying hard to pry him away from Butler, where he stayed loyal for 13 years. It was a complicated process. After all, Stevens himself brushed away several multi-million offers from other schools to stay loyal to Butler. He had previously told the media that he would coach no other college.[vi] But this was the NBA, and it was the Boston Celtics offering him their top coaching job.

Of course, Brad Stevens accepted the job but was deeply emotional about leaving Butler. Coaching in the NBA was a challenge he had long been dreaming of, but Butler and Indianapolis were home to him. He was given the opportunity to be a part of the tradition and the team 13 years ago. It was where he started his quest to become a basketball coach. It was a team he had become synonymous with for the last six seasons ever since he took over the head coaching duties. The entire team, including the staff and the executives, also felt emotional. After all, Brad Stevens was the best coach in school history and was a beloved part of the community.

Brad Stevens would make the announcement in a team meeting. Together with his wife in the locker room and with tears in both of their eyes, Brad and Tracy Stevens announced the inevitable. The then 36-year-old coach was leaving for the Boston Celtics. But while it was a sad day for Stevens and the entire Butler community, the players and staff could not help but be happy and thankful for what Stevens had given to a small school like theirs. It was a hard pill to swallow for both the Stevens family and Butler, but it was a road they had to take. Butler would continue the tradition of hiring within the family. They would replace Stevens with one of his former assistants. As for Brad Stevens, he was bound for Boston.

Chapter 3: Coaching in the NBA

Brad Stevens came to the Boston Celtics for the 2013-14 season without a lot of pressure or expectation on his shoulders. The Celtics were trying to move on from their latest Big Three era. Ray Allen had just left the team a season before to play for the Miami Heat. Paul Pierce and Kevin Garnett were both traded to the Brooklyn Nets believing it was in the best interests of the Celtics if they left to allow the team to rebuild.

What Brad Stevens was mandated to do with the Celtics was grow with the team. At 36 years old at that time, he was the youngest head coach in the NBA. He had also just inherited a team looking to get younger by rebuilding from the draft. With time to spare and with several first-round picks waiting year after year, Brad Stevens would want to grow and learn from coaching the Celtics as much as the Celtics would try to improve and learn from their new head coach as well.

Brad Stevens' first season with the Celtics was not easy. He had several veteran players in Gerald Wallace, Brandon Bass, Rajon Rondo, Jeff Green, and Kris Humphries, among others. However, he was brought in to let the younger guys grow and learn, much like how his coach back in high school asked him to come off the bench in favor of the freshmen and the sophomores. It was then and there that he understood the lesson that his high school coach had been trying to teach him back then. It was a difficult task to try and convince a former All-Star like Gerald Wallace to take a bench role. Humphries was also good enough to start for any team, but Stevens put him on the bench in favor of younger players like Jeff Green and Jared Sullinger.

What was even harder for Brad Stevens was starting the season without leader Rajon Rondo, an All-Star himself who had led the NBA twice in assists. Rondo would take nearly a year off to recover from a torn ACL, but despite not playing a single minute for

Stevens early on in the season, Rondo had nothing but respect for the new head coach. He would admire Stevens because of the way he encouraged players and because of his calm demeanor. He was not someone that enjoyed yelling at players. Instead, he would always look at the positives.[vii]

In that first season with the Celtics, Brad Stevens would work on improving the team's defense just as he did when he inherited the head coaching duties at Butler University. The Celtics would improve on their defensive rating that season, though they were still losing games due in large part to injuries and the inexperience of their young players. Nevertheless, everyone could already see that Stevens was the perfect coach to oversee the Boston Celtics' rebuilding project though he would end the season with a 25-57 record.

The following season, the Boston Celtics went on full rebuilding mode after trading away Rajon Rondo to acquire promising young forward Jae Crowder. They would also move leading scorer Jeff Green to the Memphis Grizzlies to make room for younger players on the roster. The midseason deals and the additional players had Brad Stevens struggling to adjust his lineups every single game. However, what was surprising was that his Celtics were competing very well.

The addition of 5'9" point guard Isaiah Thomas gave Brad Stevens a player he could give the ball to whenever the offense was stagnant. Thomas would come off the bench for the Celtics, but would lead the team in scoring as Stevens was still on the hunt for the perfect starting lineup. Nevertheless, the Boston Celtics won 40 out of 82 games and were on their way to the playoffs as the seventh seed in the Eastern Conference. They would ultimately get swept by the Cleveland Cavaliers in the first round. Even though the Celtics had a losing record that year, Stevens finished fourth in voting for the Coach of the Year award.

Despite getting hired to coach a rebuilding team, it would seem that Brad Stevens had already advanced the timetable set for him by the Boston Celtics after surpassing expectations season after season. The Celtics would win 48 games during the 2015-16 season. The Celtics just kept improving under Stevens as the young head coach had fully harnessed the young talent he had. But even after making the playoffs as the fifth seed, they would lose to the Atlanta Hawks in six games in the first round.

As Brad Stevens kept on improving as the Celtics head coach, so did the roster. Boston would add former All-Star center Al Horford to anchor the inside defense. They would also draft promising young rookie Jaylen Brown with the lottery pick they had. But the biggest revelation that Brad Stevens had was the emergence of Isaiah Thomas as a superstar, who finished third in the league in points per game and first among all players concerning fourth quarter scoring.

Throughout that season, Brad Stevens kept the Boston Celtics fighting hard for the top spot in the East. He was even named the head coach of the Eastern Conference All-Stars because of the consistent play of the Celtics. As the season ended, the Boston Celtics finished with the top seed in the East and with a record of 53-29. For the third straight season, Brad Stevens exceeded expectations and was growing as a coach while his team was starkly improving every single year.

Chapter 4: What Makes Brad Stevens a Good Leader

Hard Work

As they say, the way a team plays is only an extension of the coach's attitude and outlook towards the game. The team's attitude is a reflection of the coach himself. One can tell a lot about the coach just by observing how his team plays and how they look at the game of basketball. You see how calm and disciplined the San Antonio Spurs play on the court, and they reflect how calm and disciplined of a coach Gregg Popovich is. For the Golden State Warriors, the freedom and flow they play with reflect how carefree and happy-go-lucky Steve Kerr is as a person.

For Brad Stevens, the primary main trait you see from his players that perfectly reflects himself as a person is how hardworking the Boston Celtics are. Ever since he could remember, Brad Stevens had always worked hard for everything he got in his life. He was a hardworking star student and athlete back in high school. He then translated the same hard work to college where he graduated as a member of the Dean's List while owning the captainship of the DePauw Tigers during his senior year.

But the road that Brad Stevens took to get to the NBA is what shows how hardworking he is as a person. He would leave a secure corporate job in an acclaimed pharmaceutical company to follow his passions. Stevens accepted a low-paying job as a coordinator for Butler while never even complaining about the pay or how difficult the job could get. And when he became an assistant coach, he worked hard to earn the team's trust and to understand the system until he inherited the head coaching duties after six seasons.

When he coached the Butler Bulldogs, Stevens' leadership can be seen from how hard his players worked night in and night out. Brad Stevens taught the Butler Bulldogs how to work hard on the defensive end, though he was never a strong defender back when he was a player. Because of how hard his players worked on the defensive end, Stevens and the Bulldogs were able to shut their opponents down during their 2010 miracle run to the NCAA title game. Before the championship game, they had kept all of their opponents under 60 points by playing stingy and smart defense.

Even though key players such as Gordon Hayward and Shelvin Mack had left the program to become promising NBA players, the Butler Bulldogs never fell off the track under Brad Stevens' leadership. Veterans and freshmen were all playing their butts off and working hard for the sake of adding prestige to the name of the school, which managed to move to the Big East Conference after dominating their previous conference for several seasons under Stevens.

When Brad Stevens finally made the jump to the NBA to coach the Boston Celtics, he brought the same kind of mentality and culture to his team of professionals. Despite struggling during his rookie season as a head coach, it was clear that Stevens' priority was to get his players to work hard, not only in practice, but during games as well. It would take no time for him to engrave that mentality into the Boston Celtics' culture.

As early as his second season in the league, several coaches and analysts had already seen how Brad Stevens had established a culture of hard work into the Boston Celtics. Then-Indiana Pacers head coach Frank Vogel, who is known for his physical defensive strategies, recognized how hard the Celtics played. Then-Timberwolves head coach Rick Adelman, a veteran of many NBA wars, said that the Boston Celtics were competing hard under Brad Stevens. Former Celtics head coach Doc Rivers said the same thing. He stated that Brad Stevens had found a way to make a rebuilding team compete hard every night as if they were not rebuilding.[viii]

The best statement came from former NBA coach Hubie Brown. Brown would agree and reiterate what every other coach in the NBA had said about Brad Stevens and the Boston Celtics. He recognized that the Celtics, as they were that season, were not talented. They did not even have any All-Stars in the team. However, Brown said that Brad Stevens had found a way to maximize his players' talents and to make them compete hard every game. This was what former Boston player Paul Pierce calls "Celtic Pride." [viii]

But while coaches, players, and analysts alike have been giving props to Brad Stevens for making the Boston Celtics arguably the hardest working team in the entire NBA, the young head coach would rather take no credit for the work that his team has done. Brad Stevens was not only a hard working person himself, but he was also one of the most humble individuals in the league.

Brad Stevens believed that the effects that a coach has on the team as far as the work they put on the floor are overrated. What he believes is that hard work is something ingrained into the person and the player. It was either they had it, or they did not. Stevens believes that what he and the front office have done was to get players that work their butts off for the team. According to him, that kind of hard work was what kept the Celtics alive during his tenure as the head coach.[viii]

One of those hard working guys that have had the chance to play under Brad Stevens was Gerald Wallace, who spent two seasons with him. Though he was never the most skilled, the most athletic, or the biggest player on the floor, Gerald Wallace forged a respectable NBA career and was once an All-Star precisely because of how hard he works to contribute to his team. Wallace recognized that when he was with the team, the Boston Celtics had no dominant player on the roster. They were a group of five guys playing hard every single day.[viii]

Defensive guard Avery Bradley, who has been with the Boston Celtics since Brad Stevens took over as head coach, is one of the hardest working players on the roster, particularly on the defensive end where he is mostly needed. He said that, as a young team, the Celtics would have a problem battling with effort, especially when things did not go well for them. But Brad Stevens helped them in that battle.[viii]

Over time, players that have signed and have been drafted by the Boston Celtics have embraced the culture of hard work. Isaiah Thomas, who was the final draft pick of the 2011 NBA Draft, had to work his way up to relevance in the NBA. But it was not until he became a Celtic under Brad Stevens that he blossomed into a star. It was the culture of hard work that got him working harder than he ever did. And since becoming a Celtic, he has become a two-time All-Star and the team's leading scorer.

With all those said, there is no doubt in anybody's mind that Brad Stevens has engrained the nature of working hard onto the Boston Celtics' tradition. Players have embraced the value of hard work and toughness on the floor precisely because that was what Brad Stevens taught them to do. Whether or not it is in their nature to work hard is out of the question because the common denominator among all the hard working players on the Boston Celtics roster is their coach Brad Stevens.

The Butler Way

When Brad Stevens took over as the head coach of the Butler Bulldogs in 2007, he was continuing a legacy of assistant coaches getting promoted to the top coaching job in Butler. The school had long been practicing developing and hiring within the family. As such, Butler makes sure that there is continuity in the program and that the system and tradition live on, even after a new head coach takes over. One such culture and tradition that Brad Stevens continued was "The Butler Way."

The Butler Way was not coined by Brad Stevens or any of his immediate predecessors. It is a tradition and culture in Butler University that has spanned nearly a generation in its basketball program. It all started with Paul "Tony" Hinkle, who stayed with Butler for five decades as the coach of its basketball, baseball, and football programs. During his tenure, he led the Bulldogs to two NCAA basketball titles.[ix]

The legacy that Hinkle left in Butler was not the titles or wins he had amassed during his 50-year career. It was the teachings, philosophies, and culture he had passed on to his players, coaches, and other staff members that paved the way for Butler to become one of the more successful small market schools in the entire country.[ix]

Butler basketball would live on the teachings and philosophies of Hinkle for decades without even so much as codifying his words. In a sense, Hinkle's legacy lived on with the players and coaches that have learned from Hinkle. They would then pass it on to their players and assistants as decades went by. One of the people that have had the pleasure of learning Hinkle's teachings was Barry Collier, the current athletic director of Butler University.[ix]

When Barry Collier was still the head coach of the Butler Bulldogs, he would formalize all the teachings and philosophies that had been passed down by Hinkle himself. He would simplify those teachings and would create five pillars that encompassed all of what he learned from Hinkle and those who came after him. Collier would call it "Butler Way":[ix]

1.   Humility - Those who humble themselves will be exalted;

2.   Passion - Do not be lukewarm, commit to excellence;

3.   Unity - Do not divide our house, team first;

4.   Servanthood - Make teammates better, lead by giving; and

5.   Thankfulness - Learn from every circumstance.

Other than that, Butler coaches and players are also mandated to do the following:[ix]

1.   Living our core values;

2.   Placing the well-being of our teammates before individual desires;

3.   Embracing the process of growth; and

4.   Demonstrating toughness in every circumstance.

The five pillars of the Butler Way are not entirely novel considering that several teams were already practicing and embodying similar philosophies and teachings. However, what made Butler unique in their approach was the way they always made sure that their beliefs and tradition always continued from one coach to another and from one batch of players to the next.

Moreover, what sets Butler apart was that they did not develop people to learn and adjust to the Butler Way. They built their program and system around coaches and players that already embody what Butler believes in. Rather than taking the time to make coaches and players buy into the culture and tradition, Butler finds people that already are already selfless and have the team-first mindset.

Those are some of the very reasons as to how Brad Stevens kept the Butler Bulldogs competitive during his tenure as their head coach. Stevens kept the Butler Way running through the blood of his players while also making them compete harder on the floor every single game. By watching Butler games during Brad Stevens' time as the head coach, one can see how the players embodied the culture and traditions of the program.

When he was at Butler, Brad Stevens never had the most talented players on his roster. The best player he has had the pleasure of coaching was Gordon Hayward, who was chosen ninth overall by the Utah Jazz back in the 2010 NBA Draft. Other than Hayward, he has had no players that have cracked the lottery in the draft or even been drafted in the first round. The next best player that Stevens had was Shelvin Mack, who was drafted in the second round. The rest of Butler's roster was composed of hard working and selfless players that are not even talented enough to make it to the NBA.

However, it is not the talented types such as Hayward or Mack that made the Bulldogs regular contenders during Stevens' run as the head coach. It was how Brad Stevens maximized the unselfishness of those that perfectly embody the Butler Way that made the

Bulldogs back-to-back NCAA Tournament finalists. For Butler and Stevens, it was never about the talent but rather more of the mindset.

The players that have embodied the Butler Way and those that played under Brad Stevens in Butler are what Moneyball author Michael Lewis would call "No-Stats All-Star." Those are the kinds of players that look replaceable on paper because of their meager contribution to the team concerning stats. Those are the players that do not have gaudy numbers in points, rebounds, assists, steals, or blocks, and yet they are the very same ones that every championship team can do without.[ix] Brad Stevens was able to make due of the amount of "No-Stats All-Stars" he had in his Butler teams.

Expert observers of the Butler program, Craig Caldwell and Jerry Toomer, call those types of players 'catalysts.' In chemistry, a catalyst by itself is useless. But when used between two substances, it would produce a reaction that would not have happened had the catalyst been absent. Those are the kinds of players that Brad Stevens had in Butler. He had multiple catalysts that made other catalysts perform better than they would have otherwise.[ix] That kind of culture was what made Butler staples in the NCAA Tournament under Brad Stevens' leadership.

Brad Stevens would also bring the Boston Celtics the philosophies of the Butler Way. The moment Brad Stevens started coaching the Celtics, there was immediately humility, passion, unity, servanthood, and thankfulness in the way the team played night in and night out. The Celtics under Stevens remained humble in both wins and defeats. From the way they worked hard every game, the passion to compete was there. No single player dominates the team. There was always a sense of unity enveloping the Celtics. Every player on the roster worked to make others better. And best of all, the Celtics learned from their experiences every year to become better than what they were the previous season.

While the Butler Way focuses on those five pillars that Collier has coined, the point of the culture is simple: there should always be togetherness on the floor. Though the Celtics did not look like the Butler Bulldogs, who were hard-nosed defensively and kept opponents from scoring, the Butler Way was still evident in the way they play. There was always togetherness and a sense of continuity on the floor for the Celtics when Brad Stevens started coaching them. It has been an entirely different system from when Stevens was in Butler. The Bulldogs played a slow-paced defensive style while the Celtics played fast. Nevertheless, the core values of the Butler Way were always there in the two teams that Stevens coached.[x]

While the NBA and the college game are entirely different fields especially concerning competition and style, Brad Stevens was able to adjust well to the big leagues not because he was using the same system but because of his similar leadership abilities. Other than making his team work hard and compete more than they ever did, he brought with him the core values of the Butler Way that works on every organizational setup whether it be in team sports or the corporate world.

Adaptability

Brad Stevens was known for his adaptability back in Butler where he had to endure key players graduating or leaving early to pursue professional careers elsewhere, if not the NBA. He has adapted to his players year after year without sacrificing the team's system or the defensive identity that Butler has been known for during his tenure. Even when Gordon Hayward left for the NBA in 2010, Butler was still able to get to the NCAA Finals for a consecutive year on the strength of only one future NBA player named Sheldon Mack.

But Brad Stevens' adaptability showed even more than it ever had when he began coaching in the NBA. He inherited a Boston Celtics team that was rebuilding. The Celtics had bloated contracts from the trade that sent Paul Pierce and Kevin Garnett to the Brooklyn Nets. They also had several draft picks to work on while rookies and sophomore players dominated the roster.

The challenge for Brad Stevens came when the Boston Celtics front office started to make deal after deal to get rid of bloated contracts and to slowly move on from the recent Big Three era. In only the first two seasons of his career as a head coach, Brad Stevens had to work with more than 30 players that have donned the Celtics uniform. He had to make several roster and lineup adjustments and changes whenever players went in or out because they were either traded or injured.

Brad Stevens started his head coaching career with Jeff Green as his leading scorer. He also had to work with several lineup changes when Rajon Rondo was recovering from an ACL injury. At one point, he even put known chucker and bad shot taker Jordan Crawford on the starting point guard position to see how he well he works as a playmaker. And then, suddenly, those three players would get traded. The Celtics were trying to get cap space and gather more draft picks for the next few years. Because of that, nobody expected Brad Stevens to make an impact with a team that had to undergo so much transformation in a span of only two seasons.

At one point during his second year in the league, Brad Stevens had the Boston Celtics at a 20-32 record more than halfway through the regular season. The team added scoring point guard Isaiah Thomas in a trade with the Phoenix Suns. And after the trade deadline, the roster suddenly got the stability that Brad Stevens had longed for. The Celtics would go on to win 20 out of their remaining 30 games that season to make the playoffs for the first time under Brad Stevens' leadership.

That was one of the more surprising turnarounds during the 2014-15 season. It also showed how adaptable Brad Stevens is to personnel changes. Over the course of that single season, the Celtics were reported to have had a total of 40 players that have either come to or stayed with the team. One cannot help but be impressed by how Stevens was able to coach the same way he does under the circumstances of not having the same core group of starters and role players for an entire season.[xi]

Brad Stevens' adaptability is not only shown in the way he handles personnel changes and roster turnovers. He is also known for being able to adjust on the fly, even when he was still at Butler. Stevens' ability to change tactics mid game and to adapt his defense on the fly was how he was able to make the NCAA Finals twice while beating bigger programs and more established schools in the process.

Back at Butler, Brad Stevens was also known for his ability to suddenly adjust and change the way the team played in the middle of the season despite having the same group of players he started the year with. As Buzz Williams of Marquette would say, Brad Stevens does not coach the same team he does in March as the one he had in November. What Williams pointed out was Stevens' ability to make his team better in a span of just a few months. He makes the necessary adjustments depending on who they are facing while also making sure the team does not lose its identity.

Todd Lickliter, who Brad Stevens worked with as an assistant at Butler for six seasons, said that his former protégé was good at making adjustments and formulating plans on the fly. He can analyze data and see how players react to changes a lot quicker than anyone can. That has helped him become more adaptable to changes in the middle of the season or even in the midst of an actual game.[i]

Brad Stevens' smooth transition from college to the NBA also shows how well he adapted to two entirely different coaching challenges. Not only was he able to acclimate himself quickly to the NBA, which he has not even experienced as a player or as an assistant before coaching the Celtics, but he was also able to put in place in the Celtics' culture the same teachings and beliefs he lived by when he was in Butler.

There are several differences between the college game and the NBA that Brad Stevens had to work with. Other than several different rules, the NBA poses the challenge of making the coach endure difficulties such as salary cap, taxes, player egos, hands-on agents, ticket and merchandise revenues, and a more meddling media, among other things. However, Brad Stevens has not only shown that he was able to quickly adjust to such a more hectic and different kind of job, but he was also able to put his focus where it mattered the most.

For Brad Stevens, his focus was not the matters outside of the game, but the ones he could control inside. One of his first concerns and adjustments was the time difference between the NBA and the college game.[xii] The differences in game time and the shot clock meant that the NBA had more possession and in-game adjustments to work with than in college, where halves are played 20 minutes each and where the shot clock sounds after 30 seconds.

Practice time was also one of the major concerns that Brad Stevens had to adjust to. In the NBA, schedules are compressed, and teams had to play as much as four games in a week. This meant less practice time as compared to college, where Brad Stevens said that they had three training sessions for every game they played. Meanwhile, in the NBA, a team would be lucky to have a 2-1 ratio between practices and games.

Because of the less practice time he had to work with, Brad Stevens made practices and film sessions more meaningful. It was quality over quantity for him. The meager amount of practices also meant that Brad Stevens had to make adjustments quicker than he ever did when he was in college. He would say that the NBA game gives more importance to stability because of how few practices are compared to the games that a team has to play in a season.[i]

But even with the few practices sessions he has had with the Celtics in his first two seasons, Brad Stevens has shown a quick ability to make plans on the fly and adjust to personnel changes as the Celtics were still battling their way through roster stability. This speaks not only of his ability to adapt, but to his overall adaptability as a leader.

The Personality

Being calm on the sidelines has often been one of the characteristics shared among some of the NBA's greatest coaches. The most noise that the 11-time NBA champion Phil Jackson made during games was whistling to get his players' attention. Meanwhile, five-time NBA champion Pat Riley coaches games calmly and with a grin on his face, the same way that Steve Kerr does on the floor. And despite his sudden outbursts of emotions, Gregg Popovich remained as calm and composed as a military man most of the time.

While it had no effect on the strategy or plays getting run and called on the floor, the coach's calm demeanor affects the outcome of the game more than what people might think. Players would not want to see their leader bursting with emotion and rattled on the sidelines because it also affects them mentally. When the coach is the first to lose his cool, players will follow as well. It affects the psyche of the players whenever the coach fails to stay calm and collected despite getting the wrong end of the calls and the mistakes his team commits.

For Brad Stevens, it is that very same calm demeanor that has earned him the praise and respect of the players he has had the opportunity of coaching. Celtic point guard Rajon Rondo loved how Stevens remained calm and collected. He focused on showing the positives of the players rather than shoving mistakes in their faces. This was a trend that went on for Brad Stevens and the Boston Celtics even as different faces came and went.

Avery Bradley, a staple in the Boston Celtics' roster, once said that Brad Stevens always keeps his cool, even when he wanted to make a point to his players. As Bradley described, Stevens does it in a way only he could. Several of his other players have also made a claim that Brad Stevens does not humiliate nor dwell on the mistakes. He makes his point quickly, then moves on, even though several of his players have had to face issues that could have exploded. Brad Stevens does not dwell on mistakes or issues. He stays calm and would rather think of a solution than overreact.[xiii]

Brad Stevens remembered one game he had when he was coaching the Butler Bulldogs. It was his first season, and the Bulldogs started it undefeated through their first eight games. The ninth game was to be played at a challenging venue. Before the match, Stevens had been stressing about what was to come. And when game time came, he was nervous and stressed. He would scold players and officials alike. The result was Butler's first loss that season.

When Brad Stevens went over what had happened that game, he recalled how tight his players were. He thought that they were merely reflecting how tight he was throughout the entire night. Since then, Stevens made it a point never to be on edge during a game no matter what the circumstance was. He would vow to keep his cool and never to never his temper and composure during a game.[xiii]

Since coming to the NBA, he has become the subject of coaches that rave about how calm he stays. He has earned the praises of legends such as Gregg Popovich and former Coach of the Year Mike Brown, who would say that Brad Stevens even keeps his body language in check. Even when the Boston Celtics managed to win games on sideline setups that Brad Stevens himself drew up, the coach does not even celebrate as much as his players do. He just stands there on the sidelines calm as ever with a smile on his face.[xiii]

Despite that calm demeanor on the sidelines, Brad Stevens is anything but a slacker. The young head coach often gets the best out of his players by staying on them as much as he can or until his players get the message. But Stevens does it through swift action and simple words instead of inflating the bubble and letting it burst out of proportion. He never goes public with an issue or a problem he has had with one or two of his players.

Though Brad Stevens displays a calm demeanor of a quiet coach, he was always one of the better communicators, not only to his players and staff, but those outside of the team as well. Stevens communicates his message well to his players in a way only he knows how. He would even get a little hands-on during practices by making himself an extra passer or rebounder. And during media sessions, he is even able to address reporters by their first name. That action alone speaks so much of his affability as a leader. He knows how to create chemistry between himself and another person. And with that kind of ability, he can easily tell whether or not his players have the needed chemistry to win.

As Barry Collier would put it, what he believes as Brad Stevens' best asset is his ability to communicate. Stevens was always honest in the way he coaches. He makes his players know he feels and what he believes they should do to win more games. He stresses his personnel's strengths while never dwelling on mistakes and weaknesses. It is a trait that has kept him loved by the organization and its fans. It is what got him praises from coaches and players that have had the opportunity to play under him or observe how well he leads the Celtics.

And while success may get into the heads of other coaches, Brad Stevens has remained humble in doing his job. He always believes himself as an uninteresting fellow that had little stories and jokes to tell to his players. Stevens calls his daily routine boring as he only does his job and leaves it all to the players, who he believes deserves all of the credit and attention he has been getting.

The humble, hardworking kid from Zionsville, Indiana remained true to himself the moment he started coaching in Butler. He was always humble as one of his mentors once told him to be the same person he always was. Stevens never tried to change himself nor become someone he was not. He was always comfortable in his skin, and that made him humble with all the accomplishments he has earned since the moment he started coaching in Butler up until the time he made the Boston Celtics relevant again.

A Diligent Student Turned Coach

Brad Stevens was always an achieving student in the field of academics ever since he was in high school. He was one of those few students that could find the time to juggle academics with sports and other extra activities. He would eventually be a multiple-time Academic All-American nominee when he got to college, particularly because of how well he was able to shuffle his studies with his basketball activities. He would even graduate as a member of the Dean's List at DePauw University.

When he was starting as a coordinator for the Butler Bulldogs back in 2000, Brad Stevens had the same kind of diligence when he spent countless hours putting together video clips for the team to watch.

Since then, it has been an easy chore for him to watch and compile various films of plays and strategies he believes can help his team win. He is often described as a master of putting together and studying film while also systematically breaking down what he sees on tape. By spending hundreds of hours studying tape and breaking down every aspect of the game, Stevens has made it an easy task for him to find out an opponent's weaknesses and trends.

One of his former players in Butler, Ronald Nored, describes Brad Stevens as an oracle of sorts because of how well he can foresee the weaknesses and defensive lapses of their opponents well ahead of their scheduled games. He makes it easy for his players to see their opponents' tendencies and he would promptly react and find measures to take advantage of their weaknesses.[xiv]

This is an entirely different side to how Brad Stevens leads his players. On one side, he leads them through hard work, intangibles, and the way he acts towards his players. On the other side is the academic part of Brad Stevens' way of leading his team. He was always one of the most intelligent student-athletes in the country. In time, he took his intelligence and coupled it with his love and passion for the game of basketball to become a competent coach at looking at the empirical and theoretical side of the sport.

Chapter 5: How Brad Stevens Maximizes Player Talent

The Outlook on the Game

How Brad Stevens looks at the game of basketball as a coach ultimately defines who he is as a leader. Stevens has never cared so much about the results of a match or the end-of-the-season standings of his team. He would say that his emphasis and focus upon donning the head coach's mantle was towards the process and progress that his team was seeing year by year, month after month, and day after day.[xv]

But Brad Stevens was not always like that. The change in his approach and outlook has roots that dig deep into his early days as a high school prodigy in sports and academics. He would describe himself as an impatient young man that focused more on achievements and success rather on what he learned from the process and progress of going to school and playing basketball. He described himself as a "box checker" that loved crossing boxes off his checklist of accomplishments. He was afraid of making mistakes or thinking he might not be good enough for whatever endeavor he was chasing.[xiv]

But the years as an assistant coach at Butler and the wisdom he has gotten from several sources over the years have changed the way Brad Stevens approaches and sees the game of basketball. He would learn in a Stanford professor's work called "Mindset" that mindset itself and the approach that a person takes to his work is what would ultimately help him tackle problems put before him in the future.

Brad Stevens would learn from the work that those who often struggle with difficult challenges and obstacles have a fixed mindset that dwells on the ability of his natural intelligence and talents. Those are the types of people that tie achievement to their abilities. They have fixed their minds towards what they have been naturally gifted with, but would ultimately struggle whenever problems arose that proved to be harder than what their natural intelligence and talents could handle. Meanwhile, the other type of a mindset dwells on the idea that intelligence and talent can be harnessed and developed by working ➤ hard. Those kinds of people believe in the growth process of an individual, and when faced with difficult challenges, they thrive more often than not because of their belief that they can one day outgrow whatever problems they are facing.[xiv]

The growth mindset was what Brad Stevens would adopt during his time as a coach at Butler all the way to his days with the Celtics. Stevens has seen how coaches have been obsessing about ultimately chasing trophies and accomplishments instead of putting emphasis and focus on their growth and progress.[xiv] Stevens believes that living a life of focusing on effort and growth is much more enjoyable because there are no absolutes as compared to those that fixed mindset, who believe that there is only either winning or failing.

With that kind of an approach and mindset to the game of basketball, there was no wonder how Brad Stevens was able to accomplish a lot with the pieces he had when he was still with Butler.

The notion about basketball is that it is a talent-driven game. Those with natural talents and gifts would excel, dominate, and win trophies more than their less talented counterparts. But the problem for Stevens back at Butler was that he had no transcendent natural talent to work with on his teams. Butler, a mid-major school, often loses to bigger programs during recruitment. It is a team built on from players that were not top-ranked back in high school. Despite those limitations, the growth mindset that Brad Stevens has adopted allowed his players to focus more on effort and progress rather than the limitations of their natural abilities. It was how Brad Stevens made Butler the giant slayer during March Madness.

But the NBA is different from the college game. The NBA is a league dominated by superstar and transcendent talent. As opposed to college where stars can be beaten by system and teamwork, championship teams in the NBA almost always have stars to rely on. Since the dawn of the new millennium, only the 2014 San Antonio Spurs and the 2004 Detroit Pistons were able to win NBA titles without having one player averaging over 20 points. But then again the Spurs had a collection of veteran and young talents on top of having an all-time great coach. Meanwhile, the Pistons had four All-Star quality players in the prime of their careers back then.

For decades, the NBA has surrounded championship superstars with even more talent. Michael Jordan had All-Star teammates. Kobe Bryant and Shaquille O'Neal had each other. And LeBron James always had two other stars flanking him. Simply put, it is a difficult thought to form championship teams and contenders without a collection of star talent on the roster. The culture of the NBA has had a fixed mindset in determining which team would eventually walk out with the championship trophy. Rather than rewarding those that strive through effort and growth, the NBA gives emphasis to those that come out on top with talent and superstar power.

Despite that, the growth mindset has seen its share of success in the NBA. In 2004, Kobe Bryant and Shaquille O'Neal were leading the Los Angeles Lakers as favorites to win the NBA title. The two superstars had Karl Malone and Gary Payton, who had two other all-time greats flanking them though they were past their primes. But their reliance on their superstar prowess got them perplexed when the 2004 Detroit Pistons posed a defensive challenge to them that proved too much for their talents alone to crack.

The same thing happened to the 2007 Cleveland Cavaliers, who were only in the NBA Finals because of LeBron James' talent. LeBron James, flanked by two other All-Stars in 2011, was unable to beat a Dallas Mavericks team that relied on their system and teamwork more than they did on their talent. And in 2014, a group of Spurs players that stuck with a perfectly executed gameplan were able to soundly defeat the same Miami Heat team that fell to the Mavericks in 2011.

Though collections of superstar talents have shown the ability to dominate their opposition and win championship after championship in the NBA, it was never enough to rely on their abilities alone, as history would show. Having a fixed mindset truly makes it harder to solve problems that talent alone could not crack. Just ask the 2004 Lakers, who could not solve the defensive puzzle of the Pistons. Just ask LeBron James, who got outscored by Jason Terry during the 2011 NBA Finals. In essence, having a fixed mindset gets results but taking the growth mindset approach also makes a person more adaptable to change in challenging situations.

Brad Stevens took the same growth mindset approach with him when he came to Boston to coach the Celtics. Since taking over the Boston Celtics' head coaching position in 2013, Stevens had to work with a roster of players that were not as talented as the rest of the league. He inherited rookies, youngsters, and outcasts with bloated contracts when he came into Boston. It was a roster full of players that were yet to prove themselves and those that failed to do so and were branded as outcasts. He had no stars to work with, nor did he have young talent that had the potential to become transcendent.

Despite his mindset and approach to the game of basketball, even Brad Stevens admits that he and the rest of the league love those transcendent players. If given a choice, he would gladly accept a transcendent talent or two great superstars into his roster. He would also prefer shortening his rotation to a collection of about nine key players.[xiv] But then again, Brad Stevens accepted the reality of the situation.

The reality was that the Boston Celtics had no transcendent talent and that the league only has a handful of those all-time great superstars. Despite knowing how much NBA success relies on superstar players, Stevens knows that he and his team just cannot wait for one great talent to just suddenly pop out of their roster or join them through free agency. He knows that he cannot waste time waiting for that one transcendent once-in-a-lifetime talent just to come in and save the roster from its misery. Rather than doing so, he did what he was hired to do. He made due of the roster and the talent he had on his team and made them look better than they were.[xiv]

Brad Stevens realizes that everybody in the NBA has a strength that they rely on. Players are in the biggest professional league in the world for a reason—they can do something that has deemed the worthy of being in the NBA. Stevens understands that. He understands why certain players he has on his roster are in the NBA for a reason. He knows that they have elite level talents in certain aspects of the game that got them to where they were. His job was to work with his players to find those strengths together. As he would put it, "it's about soaring with your strengths as a group".[xiv]

It would not take too much time for Brad Stevens and his Boston Celtics to see the progress and results of their growth as a team. Since taking over in 2013, Brad Stevens had improved the Celtics' win-loss record year by year until 2017 when the team grabbed the top seed in the Eastern Conference heading into the postseason. While he was chosen to grow with a rebuilding team that was slated to be one of the better teams in the league in about five or more years, Stevens sped up the process and had the Celtics contending for a total in just his fourth season as the head coach.

In line with how Brad Stevens made the team grow and learn from the process, the players themselves have also developed within the system and in pace with how the coach wanted them to. He had allowed his players to become better versions of themselves from before the time that Brad Stevens took over as the coach of the Celtics. Several other journeymen have also had their best seasons under Stevens.

A known chucker and inefficient scorer whose best basketball highlight was dunking on LeBron James when he was in high school, Jordan Crawford had arguably his best time as a player when he was a Celtic for about half of the 2013-14 season before he was traded to the Golden State Warriors. Without any other point guard in the lineup due to Rondo's injury, Stevens gave Crawford the opportunity to become a playmaker though his mentality was always to score. Because of that change, Crawford had a career-best season in assists.

Jeff Green would also find that the seasons he spent under Brad Stevens would turn out to be his best ones as a player. When he was taken early in the first round of the 2007 NBA Draft, Jeff Green was a bright young player that had a knack for scoring the ball. He would, however, miss an entire season due to a heart illness. Upon returning in 2012, Green struggled to get back to form until Stevens took over a year later. Under Stevens, Jeff Green was the Celtics' leading scorer and would become a more versatile player. A natural forward that shifts between the three and the four positions, Green would sometimes even play the shooting role for Stevens in the season and a half he spent with him. His 16.9 points per game in the 82 games he played under Stevens during the 2013-14 season remains his career best as a player.

Swingman Evan Turner, who was chosen second back in the 2010 NBA Draft, has struggled to live up to his name as one of the top lottery players of his draft class. After getting traded from the Philadelphia 76ers to the Indiana Pacers, Turner struggled to find his role and identity as a player. The Boston Celtics would give him a chance in 2014. Under Stevens, Turner blossomed into an excellent all-around perimeter player that could score, rebound, assist, and defend at high rates.

Despite playing only 28 minutes a night during the 2014-15 season, Turner turned in a career-best 5.5 assists per game as one of the best passers in Stevens' lineup.

As always, Stevens was able to maximize Turner's talents by making him a passer. He failed to excel in his past teams because he could not shoot. However, Stevens cared less about his weakness and focused more on his strengths. Turner would have similar numbers the following season. And because of how well he blossomed under Brad Stevens, Evan Turner was offered a lucrative four-year contract worth 70 million by the Portland Trailblazers during the 2016 offseason. However, he would fail to recreate the magic he had under Stevens when he moved over to Portland.

The ones that benefited the most out of the process and growth-oriented mentality that Brad Stevens uses when coaching and developing his players were the ones that stayed with the team and have become key members of his rotation if not role players that have found their niche in the league.

One player in point is forward Jae Crowder. Crowder showed promise when the Dallas Mavericks drafted him back in 2012. However, he would struggle to find minutes in Dallas as veterans were more favored by the Mavericks' head coach. In only his third season in the NBA, he would be a key piece in the trade that sent Rajon Rondo to Dallas. It was when he moved to Boston when he finally found his place as part of Brad Stevens' starting lineup.

Jae Crowder would have then career bests of 14.2 points and 5.1 rebounds in his second season with the Celtics during the 2015-16 campaign. In stark contrast, he averaged 4.8 points and 2.4 rebounds in the two full seasons he played for the Mavs. Then, during the 2016-17 season, Crowder averaged 13.9 points and 5.8 rebounds while shooting a career-best 46% from the floor and nearly 40% from the three-point area. He would also become the Celtics' best defensive asset when it came to stopping bigger perimeter players. And on offense, he has shown to be a reliable shooter especially when pulling up from the corners.

It was also in the seasons under Brad Stevens that guard Avery Bradley flourished. Bradley was a remnant of the time when the Big Three of Pierce, Garnett, and Allen were still in Boston. However, he never found the opportunity to grow during that era. He was a point guard that was described as one that could not pass or shoot. Essentially, he did not have any skill that particularly stood out. The only thing he could do was to defend.

But in only his first season working under Brad Stevens, Avery Bradley averaged then career bests of nearly 15 points and four rebounds not as a point guard but as an off guard that focused more on defense. He would then grow to become a reliable offensive threat, especially from the outside, where his number suddenly shot up to nearly 40% every season. Then, during the 2016-17 season, the 6'2" guard would go on to average career bests of 16.3 points and 6.1 rebounds while shooting 46% from the floor. It was not a coincidence that Avery Bradley improved every season under Brad Stevens just as the Boston Celtics were also improving.

During the offseason of 2016, the Boston Celtics would miss out on signing Kevin Durant, but would gain a consolation prize in the form of four-time All-Star center Al Horford. Horford would become their anchor in the paint, which was an area where the Brad Stevens era of the Celtics has struggled. Teams would always take advantage of the Celtics' lack of rim protection, but Horford's presence would improve their defense in the shaded lane.

Brad Stevens would call Al Horford the consummate teammate. He was unselfish and would always play within the system of the team. Formerly a go-to-guy at the post and a high-rate rebounder for the Atlanta Hawks, Horford would spend time stretching the floor for the Celtics by hitting jumpshots as far as the three-point area. His touches at the low post and his rebounds may have dwindled down, but Al Horford improved in another aspect of the game. Under Stevens, Horford would become a primary playmaker by making passes from both the high and low posts to cutters and open teammates out on the perimeter. After averaging only 2.7 assists his entire career before coming to the Celtics, Al Horford would nearly double that amount by norming five dimes a night under Brad Stevens. Nobody was certain how much a 30-year old veteran would improve, but Stevens made use of Horford's strength as a passer to give his big man and his team a whole new offensive dimension.

But among all of Brad Stevens' key players, there is one player that stood out as far as growth is concerned. At 5'9", Isaiah Thomas had no more room to grow physically, but it was when he was traded to the Boston Celtics in the middle of the 2014-15 season that he finally found his home and a team that appreciated his skills. Not only did Brad Stevens fully utilize what Thomas could do on the offensive end, but he also allowed the tiny point guard to develop and grow even more as a player. He averaged 19 points in the 21 games he played for Boston in 2015. The following year, he became an All-Star after averaging 22.2 points and 6.2 assists. And during the 2016-17 season, he took it a notch higher by averaging 28.9 points on 46% shooting while also leading the league in fourth quarter scoring. Though credit goes to Thomas for working harder every season, how exactly did Brad Stevens get the best out of his 5'9" point guard?

Like he always does, Brad Stevens turned Isaiah Thomas into an elite star in the league by focusing on his strengths. The 5'9" point guard spends his time driving to the basket to get points up on the board with his uncanny ability to finish in contact. His three-point shot has also become a dangerous weapon over the next few seasons. But for a player as small as Thomas, one can only wonder how much punishment he could take from bigger defenders in the paint. One can also wonder how consistent he could become from deep in case his drives are taken away from him.

Brad Stevens remedied all of those and further amplified Isaiah Thomas' otherworldly scoring talents by stretching the floor with the shooter to take away defenders from the paint. Centers would have to chase Horford out on the perimeter while forwards would have to guard the wingmen at the corner. And with all the gifted passers he has on his team, Stevens has the luxury of taking Thomas off the ball and making him a catch-and-shoot player or a cutter by letting him run off multiple screens.^{xvi}

By focusing on how much more Isaiah Thomas could grow as a player and develop his strengths, Brad Stevens was able to make the most out of a player that was seen as an after-thought. From a defensive liability and a sixth man, Stevens turned Thomas into one of the most elite guards in the entire NBA. It was all because he did not rely on the fixed mindset of looking at Thomas and all of his other players' talents. Instead, Brad Stevens turned to the issue of how his players can improve and grow through effort and process. As seen from the improvements of his team and his key players, it is evident that whatever Brad Stevens is doing is working.

The beauty about how and what Brad Stevens does to maximize his players' talent also has an enormously positive effect on the Boston Celtics from an organizational and financial standpoint. Stevens was able to get the most out of players that are on mid-level and near-minimum contracts just as well as he could have had from maximum-level players. For instance, he gets the same amount of production from Jae Crowder's mediocre contract as the Memphis Grizzlies get from the $94 million they are paying Chandler Parsons. At $6.5 million, Isaiah Thomas performs better than point guards that are getting paid $20 million a year. This gives the Celtics front office a lot of flexibility during free agency period whenever they try to fill holes in Brad Stevens' roster.

With the growth mindset he has come to embrace as a coach, not only when he was with Butler, but when he moved to the NBA as well, Brad Stevens has done wonders with the personnel and the teams he has had to work with. However, with such a mindset, growth was not limited to players alone. Along the way, Brad Stevens himself was also open to growing and learning more strategies and sequences.

Brad Stevens knows and understands that his knowledge and experience of the game is far from complete. He spends hundreds of hours watching videos of not only NBA basketball, but also of college, international, amateur, and even women's leagues. He has compiled several strategies and setups that help him adjust and make plays on the fly. He sees and understands that his gameplan coming into the game might not be perfect, so he promptly makes adjustments in the middle of plays and timeouts to get his team back up. It is that kind of a mindset that helps him understand the process of adjusting, growing, and developing players and himself as well.

Chapter 6: Brad Stevens' System

When it comes to culture and attitude towards the game of basketball, Brad Stevens has led the Butler Bulldogs and the Boston Celtics by continuing and bringing with him the famed Butler Way that has been a tradition in Butler basketball for several decades already. The Butler Way focuses on how players should act and treat one another on the team rather than the systematic and strategic aspects of basketball. For Stevens, it was of utmost importance to first establish ground rules on how to act as a player and how to treat teammates and coaches alike.

Brad Stevens' system in both Butler and Boston also dwells into how he acts in front of his players and how he treats them with respect. Stevens always keeps his cool while never losing composure around his players on the belief that his personnel would also feel on edge whenever he feels nervous or emotional on the sidelines. He wants to let his players see how calm and collected he is, and in turn, he wants them to follow suit and be just as poised and composed as he is.

Willie Veasley, a member of the 2010 Butler team that went all the way to the NCAA Finals, recalls how Brad Stevens gets them hyped up during timeouts and breaks. While other coaches would scold players and fume at them for letting the other team get huge runs, Stevens would reinforce his guys by telling them how much he believed in what they could do and how much he loved them. Rather than being a stern disciplinarian, Stevens acts like a concerned father to his team.[xvii]

However, Stevens not only acts that way during games, but also in team practices and other activities. He never scolds his players during practices, but would rather chastise them without humiliating them or to making them feel bad about themselves. One case in point was when he was at Butler, one of his best players, Ronald Nored, would kick the ball over to the bleachers because of a bad practice. Rather than scolding him or humiliating him in front of the other players, Stevens would order Nored to run laps around the team's practice facility until he believed that the player had learned his lesson. It is those simple gestures that make Brad Stevens such a respectable and effective leader. On the intangible aspect of basketball, it is one of those things that gets his system going.

Player development and maximization were always parts of what has made Brad Stevens' coaching system so effective, not only at Butler, but also in the NBA. Stevens relies on a growth mindset whenever he tries to develop his players. He believes that those who rely on such a mindset tend to be able to solve difficult problems easier than others because of their openness to change and because of their reliance on effort and development. It has been this mindset that has made the Celtics an ever improving team season by season.

Seldom does Brad Stevens rely on the fixed mindset of focusing mainly on the talents of his players. Instead, he focuses on how to develop his personnel and make them grow through process and effort. He looks at the strengths of his players and focuses on those traits rather than on the aspects he knows his players cannot excel at. Because of that, he can further develop his players on the basis of their strengths while also maximizing what they could do on the floor because of how he focuses on where his personnel excels.

Though Brad Stevens is described as a coach who leads through his demeanor, outlook, and philosophies, he is anything but limited to the intangibles and the development aspect of the game of basketball. If anything, Brad Stevens is an even better coach when it comes to the X's and O's and the strategic side of basketball because of his natural intellect and feel for the game.

The main thing in common between all the teams that Brad Stevens has coached in both college and the NBA is how hard they play defensively. Everything about Brad's system starts with the fundamentals of defense. It was how he led Butler to back-to-back NCAA Finals appearances while limiting big name programs throughout the Tournaments. And, when he came to Boston, he has steadily improved upon the Celtics' defensive efficiency year after year. How he does it is through six basic philosophies he calls the DNA of Defense:[xviii]

1. Commitment

   This is what Brad Stevens first demands from his players. He asks them to stay committed to what they believe in the system and what the coach is selling to them. It is the same commitment that the Butler Way embodies. It requires you to have the mindset of being a great, unselfish, and hardworking teammate that believes in his capabilities and strengths.

One of the ways that Brad Stevens gets his players committed on the defensive end is to challenge them. In one of Isaiah Thomas' early games with the Boston Celtics when he first joined the team, Brad Stevens gave him the assignment to guard Steph Curry of the Golden State Warriors. While he was not able to shut Curry down, he did a good job in keeping with the MVP. Since then, every time Thomas struggles or complains about his defense, Stevens reminds him of the job he did against Curry and would challenge him to do the same.

Back in Butler, he would constantly get on Ronald Nored's back by challenging his best defender to guard the opposing team. He makes it a focus to point out how Nored would sometimes struggle to guard certain players he often overlooks. At one point, Nored struggled to defend little known Isaiah Canaan in one of Butler's games. During the next huddle, Brad

Stevens would challenge his best defender by asking the entire team if Nored could guard anybody out there on the floor.[xiii] In turn, the young player answered the challenge.

2. Positioning

This aspect of Stevens' defense has always been common in any of the teams he has coached. This means stopping transition baskets over at the other end by getting back to the proper position. Stay in front of the ball, protect the painted area, and guard the wings for any transition three-pointers that teams may want to shoot.

3. Prioritizing

Brad Stevens plants it in his players' mind to prioritize stopping the other team from scoring. He does so by scouting player and team tendencies himself and by giving pointers to his teams on how to counteract any offense the opposing team might try to pull off. Stevens also challenges his players to scout the opposing team themselves and to make it a point to know the DNA of their defensive assignments.

4. Awareness

This part of Brad Stevens' defensive philosophy dwells into the mindset and unconscious psyche of his players. Stevens believes that players should be able to reach an unconsciously competent defensive awareness, wherein it has already been ingrained into your DNA and your tendencies that you already know what to do on the defensive end without even realizing it in the first place.

For Stevens, this level of competency on the defensive end allows a player to see what is going to happen next and how he should react to it without even giving a thought about it because of the force of habit, which stems from repetition, drills, practices, and proper preparation every game.

5. Execution/Technique

   Ask any coach of any team, and they would all say that execution and technique are the two most important aspects of a defensive strategy. Technique is the part that can be taught and ingrained into the players' mindset and body of work through practice, drills, film sessions, and proper coaching. The execution part stems from a coach's ability to make his players understand the importance of doing things the proper way. He must make them understand how important it is to properly box a man out, close out on shooters, and read the driving lanes. The little things matter, and it all boils down to the proper execution of every defensive play.

6. Completion

   You may have the commitment to stop your assignment from scoring and the proper positioning to stop transition baskets. You may prioritize having the proper defensive awareness. And you may execute defensive techniques to perfection. But any defensive possession can never be fully realized without completion. This means getting the defensive rebounds to complete a defensive play. Defense does not end in making your opponents miss. It ends by grabbing the rebound to stop the other team from getting an extra opportunity.

As basic as it all sounds, those six philosophies of defense are what made Brad Stevens an indispensable coach both in Butler and in Boston. He turned a Butler team that had little to no talent into a top defensive team in the nation by ingraining into them his six philosophies on defense. And in the NBA, Stevens has even earned the praise of players such as LeBron James and Kyrie Irving for the defensive work he has done with the Celtics, who made it difficult for the Cleveland Cavaliers to sweep them back in the 2015 playoffs. Stevens made it a chore for the two stars to score on them, and that was what made James and

Irving believe in how good of a defensive strategist Stevens is.

The offensive end is where Brad Stevens works a lot of his magic as a basketball genius. When he came to the Boston Celtics, one of the basic offensive philosophies he got his team to believe in was to play a fast pace and to get as many possessions as they could. In 2016, the Boston Celtics ranked fifth in the league in scoring despite not shooting as well as any of the top scoring teams in the league. In 2017, they were seventh in scoring while staying near the middle of the pack concerning overall shooting percentage from inside and outside the perimeter.

In 2016, Brad Stevens quickened the pace by relying on his team's ability to rebound the ball on the offense. While the Celtics that season were not as dominant as other teams on the boards, Stevens was able to get his players committed to gang rebound the ball and outhustle their opponents. Boston would rank third that season in offensive rebounding and would end up with the fourth-fastest pace in the NBA.

It was entirely different the following season for Stevens and the Celtics. The Celtics would focus less on the rebounding end of the floor because of the spacing the team had on the floor to free up shooters and driving lanes for their guards. Everybody on the floor could shoot the ball. On top of that, all of the Celtics were willing passers and playmakers. Stevens would also focus on more ball movement, which resulted in making the Celtics the fourth highest team concerning assists per game.

The Boston Celtics' offense revolves around their guards, notably Isaiah Thomas. Stevens, whenever Thomas has the ball, would run a lot of pick and rolls for the All-Star point guard, who would then be skilled enough to finish in the basket or to pass out to a rolling man in case the opposing big man would hedge on him to take away driving lanes. Stevens also utilizes the pick and pop as frequent as the roll because of how many shooters he has on the floor. Even center Al Horford would pop out on the perimeter for long open shots.

In essence, Brad Stevens utilizes the pace and space style that has been so often used in today's NBA where shooters are given more importance than ever before. He lets his teams space the floor so well while making sure they get as many possessions as they could. And even without Isaiah Thomas and the rest of the starters out on the floor, Brad Stevens has been able to make use of a bench that could do as much damage as the core group does because they could also run and space the floor so well.[xix]

From the time he started with the Celtics in 2013 all the way today's incarnation of the Boston team, Brad Stevens has always used space and the three-point shot to his advantage. Back then, he had David Lee and Brandon Bass popping out to the midrange to shoot jumpers. He then had Jared Sullinger rolling to the basket. Now, he has Al Horford and Kelly Olynyk hitting three-point bombs from the top of the key while Amir Johnson is a steady choice as a roller to the basket. Meanwhile, guards and swingmen are out there on the floor to give as much space for ballhandlers to drive to the basket. In such as simple offensive setup, Brad Stevens is given several options: the drive off the pick, an open shot to the roller or the popper, and the three-point shot to floor spacers.

As basic as Stevens' offensive system seems to be, what shows his genius as a head coach is his expertise in setting up out-of-bounds plays. Brad Stevens spends so much time watching film on out-of-bounds plays that he has already memorized to heart practically all of the sets he has watched in all levels of basketball. As center Kelly Olynyk would put it, Stevens spends as much as 25 hours of watching plays that last only three seconds. It does not take a math wizard to figure out how many three-second plays can fit in 25 hours of film.

Brad Stevens designs so many out-of-bounds plays during timeouts and dead ball situations that he has already formed hybrids of plays he has watched countless times. Back when the Boston Celtics faced the Cleveland Cavaliers in the 2015 playoffs, defender Iman Shumpert spent so much time watching films on Brad Stevens' out-of-bounds plays that he had already memorized them. But when game time came, he could not figure out which plays Stevens was calling because the coach had already mapped out new ones on the fly.[xiii] On any level of basketball, Brad Stevens has already become one of the best at mapping out out-of-bounds plays.

In simple terms, the beauty of Brad Stevens' system stems out from his reliance on the fundamentals of defense, where he demands his players to live by his six defensive pillars, and of offense, which is a simple reliance on space and pace and pick-and-rolls. However, Stevens was able to compound the success of his basketball system because of the intangibles such as work ethic, attitude, and outlook towards the game itself. He has instilled so many intangibles to his team to the point that his contributions and his success as a coach cannot be quantified even by a guy like him, who relies so much on the statistical and data analysis.

Chapter 7: Key Takeaways

Work Ethic

From his humble beginnings in the small town of Zionsville, Indiana, all the way to his days as the head coach of the Boston Celtics, what characterized Brad Stevens was not his genius as a player or as a coach. It was the hard work he has put into every craft he has worked on ever since he was in high school up until he was given the job to coach one of the most storied franchises in NBA history.

As a student-athlete, Brad Stevens devoted his time to do well in his academics while starring in Zionsville High School's basketball team. He put in the same amount of work on his studies that he did on his basketball skills. Stevens would continue this trend to college. At DePauw University, Stevens was a role player that devoted his basketball time as a leader for his team. Nevertheless, he never forgot to work hard on his studies as he graduated a member of the Dean's List and a multiple-time nominee of the Academic All-America.

His work ethic would translate to the coordinator job he was offered by then Butler head coach Thad Matta. In a span of only a year, he would become an assistant under new head coach Todd Lickliter. With the proper attitude and work ethic, Stevens was named the head coach of the Butler Bulldogs at the tender age of 31 years old.

As the head coach of the Bulldogs, he instilled into the team the same kind of work ethic that has gotten him to the dance. The Butler Bulldogs started to become more fierce on the defensive end. They were scrappy hard workers that competed on every single play without forgetting to play smart on both ends of the floor just as their coach never forgot to stay sharp while working hard on his endeavors.

The same could be said about the Boston Celtics. Brad Stevens inherited a group of misfits when the franchise sought to rebuild from scratch. Despite coaching rookies, sophomores, and castaway players that other teams did not like, Stevens was able to get his team to play harder than they ever did. The result was a playoff appearance for a team that did not have any stars and one that relied chiefly on Avery Bradley, Evan Turner, Brandon Bass, Jared Sullinger, and an Isaiah Thomas that was yet to break out.

The amount of work that Brad Stevens puts into his craft is also maniacal. He spends hundreds of hours watching films of plays from every level of basketball. He has mastered the art of mapping out plays because of the amount of time he spends to study data, film, and statistics. And because of such a work ethic, his teams followed suit. Stevens' players would put in the same amount of hard work and dedication to their craft and on the games they played that one conclusion can be gleaned—Brad Stevens' work ethic rubbed off on them.

Believing in the Organizational Philosophy

A good leader knows how to make his people buy into the philosophy and beliefs he is trying to sell to them. Brad Stevens was able to do so at both Butler and Boston by selling them the philosophies of the Butler Way, which was what made Butler basketball successful as a mid-major program slaying bigger and more established schools in the process.

Butler basketball has always lived by the mantra of the Butler Way, which has paved the way for the school to succeed in college basketball. It was Brad Stevens who took it a step further by not only living the organization's mantra but by also finding the right pieces and players that already unconsciously embody what Butler basketball stands for.

It was more of the same for the Boston Celtics when Brad Stevens started coaching them. Stevens gathered around players and personnel that believed in the organizational setup and what the Boston Celtics played for. In a sense, Stevens took with him to Boston the Butler Way and allowed his players to live by it and buy into the whole team aspect that his philosophies preach.

In a sense, the Butler Way not only applies to basketball or sports, but also in any organization. In business and the corporate world, there is always a burning desire to succeed and to achieve success. But it is not only enough to ally yourself with people that love playing and working with the team. What the Butler Way teaches the world of business is that one should always surround himself with people that do not only work well with a team but are willing to sacrifice their goals and selfish desires for the betterment of the group and the organization. As Brad Stevens had multiple catalysts in Butler and Boston, one should also surround himself with people that make others around them better as a catalyst should. This very same foundation was what made Butler University successful in its right, and anyone who believes in the organizational setup can also do well with living by the core principles of the Butler Way.

The Growth Mindset

Brad Stevens' view on the way a coach should lead is not constrained by the results he sees or the achievements he gets. Stevens has never focused on how many wins or trophies the Butler Bulldogs get, or how long until he gets the eighteenth banner up on the rafters of Boston's TD Garden. What he was always focused on was on how much his teams and his players learn and develop through the process. He believes in the growth mindset more than he does on the fixed mindset.

The growth mindset is one where a person can get over difficult challenges easier by learning through effort, hard work, and development. Meanwhile, a fixed mindset entails that a person ties success with his natural skills and talents, and if ever faced with a difficult task, he or she quickly folds, believing that what tools he was given are not enough to get him over the challenge.

By believing in the growth mindset, Brad Stevens was able to overcome whatever limitations his players have as far as talent would go. Instead, he focused on their strengths and let them grow from there. And on the team setup, Stevens was always more concerned about how much his team learns season after season instead of just looking at the number of wins or trophies they may have garnered from their last campaign.

The beauty of not seeing success as one tied down to natural talents and skills but instead on how much a person can grow over time by learning and through effort can be gleaned from how Brad Stevens has steadily improved his teams year after year. It is a mentality that is not tied down by limitations of a person's talents but by how much a person can achieve through perseverance and hard work.

And while anyone would always want to be surrounded and to work with transcendent talents, there are only so much of them to go around not only in the NBA but also in any organizational setup. But just because you do not have the talent that is needed to achieve it does not mean that you are doomed to fail. Talent may be essential, but one can always achieve more by learning through effort and following the process.

Conclusion

Brad Stevens' journey to the NBA is not exactly storybook. He was not some prodigious talent that was waiting in the wings to save a struggling and rebuilding basketball team. He was not a transcendent basketball talent that learned the ins and outs of basketball from the many wars he has faced in the NBA. He was not even good enough to get a Division I scholarship let alone an NBA contract. Stevens did not even have enough connections to land him a job with one of the best coaches in the NBA.

Instead, Brad Stevens started small from the equally peaceful town of Zionsville, Indiana. What kept him going was his passion for basketball, but what made him get to where he is right now was how hard he worked. He would eventually get the head coaching job of Butler and then the Boston Celtics, but not because of the way he made use of big name talents or superstars. He did it by making everyone in his teams better by also letting them work as equally hard as he did in his life.

Brad Stevens' story is one focused on hard work and having the proper mentality and approach to improving one's craft and everyone else around him. He does not have that sense of mystique that Phil Jackson has as a coach nor does he have the uncanny mind and natural leadership skills of a Gregg Popovich. However, Stevens has commanded respect and praise in the NBA through the hard work and dedication that exudes not only from him but his teams as well. And through it all, he and the Boston Celtics have maintained the proper poise and mentality that was always needed of them to succeed in the league.

While Brad Stevens is yet to see and experience the amount of success of championship coaches such as legends Phil Jackson, Gregg Popovich, Pat Riley, and Larry Brown among others, he has already proven himself to be one of the better leaders in the league.

This is not only because of his bright strategic mind, but because of the way he gets the best out of players that seemed to be outcasts or misfits in the NBA.

From what Stevens had already displayed with the talent level he has in Boston, he is only a superstar free agent or a once-in-a-generation talented draft pick away from showing the entire world how much his style and his approach to the basketball can spell the difference between winning and losing. He may not value wins as much as the lessons his teams learn. But when the time and opportunity comes for him to grab a championship trophy by the hand, Brad Stevens would surely know what to do as seen from how he was able to do so much with so little that he had in both Butler and Boston.

Final Word/About the Author

I was born and raised in Norwalk, Connecticut. Growing up, I could often be found spending many nights watching basketball, soccer, and football matches with my father in the family living room. I love sports and everything that sports can embody. I believe that sports are one of most genuine forms of competition, heart, and determination. I write my works to learn more about influential athletes in the hopes that from my writing, you the reader can walk away inspired to put in an equal if not greater amount of hard work and perseverance to pursue your goals. If you enjoyed *Brad Stevens,* please leave a review! Also, you can read more of my works on *Steve Kerr, Gregg Popovich, Roger Federer, Novak Djokovic, Andrew Luck, Rob Gronkowski, Brett Favre, Calvin Johnson, Drew Brees, J.J. Watt, Colin Kaepernick, Aaron Rodgers, Peyton Manning, Tom Brady, Russell Wilson, Michael Jordan, LeBron James, Kyrie Irving, Klay Thompson, Stephen Curry, Kevin Durant, Russell*

Westbrook, Anthony Davis, Chris Paul, Blake Griffin, Kobe Bryant, Joakim Noah, Scottie Pippen, Carmelo Anthony, Kevin Love, Grant Hill, Tracy McGrady, Vince Carter, Patrick Ewing, Karl Malone, Tony Parker, Allen Iverson, Hakeem Olajuwon, Reggie Miller, Michael Carter-Williams, John Wall, James Harden, Tim Duncan, Steve Nash, Draymond Green, Kawhi Leonard, Dwyane Wade, Ray Allen, Pau Gasol, Dirk Nowitzki, Jimmy Butler, Paul Pierce, Manu Ginobili, Pete Maravich, Larry Bird, Kyle Lowry, Jason Kidd, David Robinson, LaMarcus Aldridge, Derrick Rose, Paul George, Kevin Garnett, Chris Paul, Marc Gasol, Yao Ming, Al Horford, Amar'e Stoudemire, DeMar DeRozan, Isaiah Thomas, Kemba Walker and Chris Bosh in the Kindle Store. If you love basketball, check out my website at claytongeoffreys.com to join my exclusive list where I let you know about my latest books and give you lots of goodies.

Like what you read? Please leave a review!

I write because I love sharing the stories of influential coaches like Brad Stevens with fantastic readers like you. My readers inspire me to write more so please do not hesitate to let me know what you thought by leaving a review! If you love books on life, basketball, or productivity, check out my website at claytongeoffreys.com to join my exclusive list where I let you know about my latest books. Aside from being the first to hear about my latest releases, you can also download a free copy of *33 Life Lessons: Success Principles, Career Advice & Habits of Successful People*. See you there!

Clayton

References

[i] Brown, Clifton. "Former Butler Coach Brad Stevens Calmly Leads Celtics Through Playoff Storms". *Indy Star.* 5 May 2017. Web

[ii] Holmes, Baxter. "Indiana Roots Bounds Brad Stevens to Basketball". *Boston Globe.* 27 October 2013. Web

[iii] MacMullan, Jackie. "Brad Stevens' Story Isn't Storybook". *ESPN.* 22 November 2013. Web

[iviv] Schlabach, Mark. "Stevens Second-Youngest Division I Head Coach". *ESPN.* 6 August 2007. Web

[v] Beaven, Stephen. "Taking a Veteran Approach to the Job of a Young Lifetime". *New York Times.* 5 January 2008. Web

[vi] Keefer, Zak. "The Day That Rocked Butler: Story Behind Brad Stevens' Departure for Celtics". *USA Today.* 25 October 2013. Web

[vii] Buckley, Zach. "Rajon Rondo on Brad Stevens: 'Who Doesn't Want to Play for a Coach Like That?'". *Bleacher Report.* 14 December 2013. Web

[viii] O'Connor, Padraic. "Brad Stevens' Culture of Hard Work Paying Off For Celtics". *Celtics Life.* 24 December 2013. Web

[ix] Belzer, Jason. "Why Butler Basketball Holds The Key To Organizational Success". *Forbes.* 7 February 2013. Web

[x] Gibbs, Grant. "Brad Stevens and The Butler Way are Evolving to Fit the NBA". *USA Today.* 20 November 2014. Web

[xi] Riaf, Ian. "Why Brad Stevens Is So Valuable". *Fan Sided.* 30 July 2016. Web

[xii] Beck, Howard. "Celtics Coach Brad Stevens: Adjusting to the NBA is a Matter of Time". *Bleacher Report.* 17 October 2013. Web

[xiii] MacMullan, Jackie. "Isaiah Thomas: Brad Stevens Could Be One of the Greatest Coaches Who Ever Lived". *ESPN.* 26 April 2016. Web

[xiv] Witz, Bill. "Butler's Coach: Competitiveness Wrapped in Calm". *New York Times.* 28 March 2010. Web

[xv] Flannery, Paul. "Brad Stevens is the Celtics' Biggest Reason for Hope". *SB Nation.* 28 October 2015. Web

[xvi] Clark, Jeff. "How Brad Stevens' "College Style" Created a Pro Star in Isaiah Thomas". *Celtics Blog.* 25 April 2017. Web

[xvii] Moore, David Leon. "Season to Dream: Butler Joins Big Boys in Indy for Final Four". *USA Today*. 28 March 2010. Web

[xviii] Benjamin, Daniel. " Brad Stevens' Defensive DNA and 6 Non-Negotiables To Success". *Breakthrough Basketball*. Web

[xix] Siegel, Jeff. "The Wizard of Boston". *Fan Sided*. 27 January 2016. Web

53080967R00077